The Buddha's Guide to Football

Bringing Mindfulness to the Game

Table of Contents

Chapter 1. Introduction

Enlightenment meets the end zone in our Special Report: "The Buddha's Guide to Football: Bringing Mindfulness to the Game". Venture with us on an enlightening journey, as we connect the ancient wisdom of Buddha to modern turf wars, drawing parallels that will invigorate your game plan and elevate your appreciation of football. Combining mindfulness techniques with gameplay strategies, this report offers a fresh perspective and practical tools to augment your performance and enjoyment of the game. It's more than just a playbook, it's a new philosophy for players, fans, and anyone looking to incorporate mindfulness into their everyday lives. You'll leave not only fascinated but also inspired, ready to bring a touch of Zen to your next football experience! So hurry, secure your copy today and embark on your own journey to enlightened football mastery.

Chapter 2. The Gridiron and the Garden: Exploring the Connection

The game of football and Buddhism, at first glance, seem like completely unrelated entities. Yet, upon deeper exploration, one might find profound similarities. The Gridiron, a reference to the football field with its grid-like markings, and the Garden, symbolic for the tranquil space where Buddha attained enlightenment, emerge as platforms where physical engagement intertwines with mental and spiritual evolution.

2.1. The Dichotomies at Play

The gridiron is understood as a charged space, where physical dominance, strategy, and the will to win clash in a finite timeline. The field, divided into a grid, signifies competition, territory, and conquest. Contrarily, the garden is perceived as a tranquil place. It denotes space for meditation, introspection, and wisdom. Together, these two seemingly contradictory spaces intertwine to form a unique perspective. Just as Buddha, in the serenity of the garden, found enlightenment, football players, amidst the tumult of the gridiron, can find their own moments of clarity and growth.

Key aspects of Buddhism can be incorporated into football. The first is the idea of 'impermanence'. In football, as in life, nothing is permanent. A leading team might be heading for a loss the very next instant, or a football player's career might get abruptly ended due to injury. Embracing this reality helps mentally condition players for the unexpected, fosters resilience, and hones their adaptability.

2.2. The Middle Way and Balancing Duality

Buddhism talks about the 'Middle Way'—a balanced approach to life, avoiding extremes. On the field, this translates into maintaining equilibrium between aggression and defense, strength and flexibility, competition and sportsmanship. Balancing this duality promotes a comprehensive approach to the game, ensuring holistic development of players. It prevents overindulgence in a single facet, which frequently leads to adverse game outcomes or injuries.

Football strategies echo this balance. A balanced offensive-defensive strategy is ideal for consistent performance. A team fully focused on offense might score high, but without a solid defense, they leave themselves open to counterattacks. Similarly, a team overly dedicated to defense might ward off many attacks but will struggle to score and win. The middle way, a balanced offensive-defensive strategy, ensures sustainability and long-term success.

Mindfulness, a cornerstone of Buddhism, is also crucial in the gridiron's high-pressure environment. It enables players to be mentally present, focused, and aware of their surroundings, leading to precise decision-making and optimal outcomes. It aids in regulating emotions and reactions, thereby preventing impulsive actions that often lead to penalties or unnecessary risks.

2.3. The Karma Factor

Karma, another key concept in Buddhism, is a potent tool on the gridiron. Your actions come with consequences. Every play you make has ripple effects for both your team and the opponent. A player's decisions contribute to the collective Karma of the team; a poorly executed play could lead to a lost match, while a well-thought-out move might secure a victory. This instills a sense of responsibility and encourages players to strive for excellence.

2.4. Mindfulness in Training and Execution

Mindfulness extrapolates well into the training regimes for football. Incorporating mindfulness-based training can enhance concentration, limit distractions, and improve decision-making on the field. It allows players to create a mental landscape where they can anticipate various scenarios, form adaptive strategies, and execute them with precision.

Game execution is a dynamic process where instants of opportunity must be seized. The constant awareness cultivated through mindfulness helps in recognizing these moments and responding intuitively. With each snap of the ball, players must be fully present, aware of their position, the opponents' movements, and the open spaces on the field. This mindfulness and presence can also help alleviate performance anxiety, promoting equanimity even under extreme pressure.

The understanding of Buddhism concepts and their confluence with football provide not just strategic insights but also a holistic approach to the game. It fosters a culture of mindfulness, balance, and insightful action that elevates the game beyond physical conquest to a realm of mental and spiritual experience and growth. The connection between the gridiron and the garden is an exploration of this very possibility. On the football field, as in the tranquil gardens of Buddhism, lessons of life and self-realization unfold. Adapting this mindfulness into the game opens avenues for enhanced performance, personal development, and a deeper appreciation for football's multifaceted nature.

Chapter 3. Buddha's Threading the Needle: Precision in Football

In weaving the intricate tapestry of football, the players, akin to skilled artisans, display their exceptional skills and facilitate crowd-roaring moments on the pitch. The roles of accuracy, precision, timing, and calmness, which define the success in threading a needle, are no different from those which channel victory in a football match. Football and mindfulness—two seemingly contrasting domains—merge in an exquisite fashion as we blend Buddha's teachings into the mechanics of the game.

3.1. The Football - Karma Connection

The concept of karma, central to Buddha's philosophy, can reflexively influence a football game. In this context, karma connotes the consequences of a player's actions during a game. On the pitch, every pass, every dribble, every tackle—these actions are the causes. The results or effects—the goals scored, the fouls conceded—are direct consequences of these causes. Just as Buddha's teachings encourage ethical actions to garner positive karma, precise and calculated actions on the field yield a fruitful outcome, a goal, a win.

3.2. Mindfulness in Passing

In football, passes are the skeleton that structures the team's movement. Much like threading the needle, successful passes require precision and keen attention. Each pass forms the foundation for another player's action, hence the importance of the quality of the pass. Dominant teams are often those who have consistently accurate and precise passes that make the opponent's attempt at regaining control grievous.

Buddha's wisdom urges us to be totally present in the current moment, focusing entirely on the situation at hand. Applying this in football, it implies imbuing each pass with absolute concentration, observing the position of teammates and opponents, the trajectory of the ball, and the receiving player's motion.

3.3. The Essence of Kokoro

The Japanese word "Kokoro" loosely translates to "heart". It embodies more than just the physical organ—it encapsulates the mind and spirit in unity. Footballers often discuss "playing with heart", however, Kokoro advocates for one to play with heart, mind, and spirit, in unison.

Kokoro is the foundation of every powerful free kick, every decisive penalty, and every exquisitely threaded through ball. Playing with Kokoro means playing with a sense of fully integrated purpose, or a singular focus that unites physical, mental, and emotional energies toward achieving a goal. It is akin to threading a needle in perfect alignment with the intention of creating a remarkable piece of art.

3.4. Equanimity in Dribbling

Dating back to Buddha, the term "Upeksha," or equanimity, describes a state of even-mindedness or a deep tranquility that remains unperturbed by the eight worldly conditions of gain and loss, fame and disrepute, praise and scorn, pleasure and pain.

Relating this to football, equanimity is an essential trait in dribbling. A player demonstrating equanimity remains calm and composed despite the adversarial players blocking their path, the crowd's intense pressure, or the ticking game clock. This tranquility permits a player to see the field clearly, enabling them to make split-second decisions that can change the games' course.

3.5. The Role of Prajna in Tactics

"Prajna" or wisdom is an inherent aspect of Buddhist teachings. In football, a player's prajna translates to their understanding of the game, their ability to read plays, and assess situations on the pitch, embodying individual and team tactics.

Football tactics can be analogized with the Buddhist Eightfold Path, where right view, right intention, right speech, right action, right livelihood, right effort, right mindfulness, and right concentration contribute to the path of enlightenment. Similarly, coordinated movements, observant defence, assiduous offenses, managed tempo, advantageous set-pieces, player teamwork, match awareness, and demonstrated capabilities weave the route to victory.

3.6. Conclusion: The Path of Righteousness in Football

As we delve deeper into the delicate balance of precision in football, drawing parallels from Buddha's teachings, it's evident how mindfulness can revitalize not just the approach towards the game, but also its execution. Like threading the needle, where the success lies in the harmony of precision and patience, in football too, mastering the game involves uniting tactical understanding, precision in execution, and a mindful presence. This unique amalgamation, akin to Buddhist Eightfold Path, can lead to the path of righteousness in football – a balanced, skilful game that flows seamlessly with grace and creativity, leading to success both on and off the pitch.

Chapter 4. Stillness Amid the Scuffle: Harnessing Inner Peace in Play

Football is a game of constant movement, rigorous dynamics and high energy. Amid the thunderous roar of the crowd, the authoritative blast of the referee's whistle, and the immense pressure of competition, how does one find peace? But the wisdom of Buddha shows us that finding inner calm in the most tumultuous situations is not only possible but can also greatly enrich our experiences and performance. In this chapter, we will discover how to harness the transformative power of mindfulness to achieve inner peace during play and apply this serene energy to our football strategies.

4.1. The Art of Mindful Movement

The Buddha says, "Just as a candle cannot burn without fire, men cannot live without a spiritual life." This applies even to physical activities like football. In every strategic run, tactical dodge, or decisive score, there's an undercurrent of spiritual energy. The first step to harnessing this energy is mindful movement.

Masters of the ancient art of Tai Chi seek to harness their 'chi' or 'life energy.' They achieve this by performing slow, deliberate movements while maintaining a heightened sense of their bodies' movements and positions. Similarly, in football, every snap, pass, and tackle can become a moment of mindfulness.

Try to feel the energy coursing through your body as you sprint across the field. Pay attention to the sensation of your muscles contracting and expanding, your foot striking the ground, and the grip of your fingers around the ball. Instead of viewing these actions as purely physical, aim to imbue them with intention and awareness.

The act of running is no longer just a means to reach the end zone but becomes a dance of energy and mindfulness.

Let's not forget that in harnessing our inner peace, we're not pursuing a solitary journey. It is about moving in sync with our team, using the breath to mirror the heartbeat of our combined effort. Such mindfulness forges better connections and improves team coordination but, most importantly, it fosters a bond that transcends mere gameplay to be a dance of unity that brings precision and focus.

4.2. Finding Your Focal Point

Staying mentally focused can be challenging when chaos beckons on the field. But in the storm, you must find your calm. To do this, pinpoint a focal object, action, or mantra to turn your attention inward.

A focal point could be anything: the rhythm of your breathing, the tightening of your shoe laces, or a mantra like "here and now." Every time your thoughts scatter, gently redirect them to your chosen focal point. This practice doesn't turn off the noise but tunes your mind to a frequency of stillness amidst the clamor.

4.3. Balancing Emotion on the Field

Football is a game of passions. It carries a whole spectrum of emotions: joy, frustration, disappointment, and determination. Allowing these emotions to control you can lead to poor decisions, aggressive behavior, and ultimately, a dip in performance.

Buddhist teachings advise observing the emotion, accepting its presence, but not becoming it. Imagine standing at the side of a road watching cars pass by - the cars are your emotions and you are the observer. You acknowledge each one without jumping in and letting it sweep you away.

Next time you feel frustration surging within you after a missed opportunity, consciously shift your perspective to that of the observer. Understand this feeling is not permanent and it certainly doesn't define you or your game. This ability to detachedly observe and let go of negative emotions can greatly increase your resilience, both on and off the field.

4.4. The Breath: Your Anchor in Chaos

In football, as in life, moments can escalate quickly. During turbulent times, the breath serves as an anchor. It is always there, a rhythmic reminder of life and calm. Pay attention to the rise and fall of your breath before snapping into action. Even in the midst of a heated play, take a moment to align yourself using your breath.

A simple yet effective technique to regain your calm amidst the hustle is 'box breathing.' Inhale deeply to a count of four, hold your breath for the same count, then exhale for a count of four. Hold again before the next inhaling breath. Visualizing this as a square or 'box' helps maintain focus on the breath and allows for mental reset, preparing the mind for the next play.

Football is more than a game of strength, speed, and strategy. It's a test of character, a journey of self-discovery, and an opportunity for growth. By applying mindfulness techniques to football, we can bring balance and serenity to the game. Whether you're a player, a spectator, or a lover of both the game and life's deeper meanings, let Buddha's wisdom guide your journey on and off the field. Let your next game not only be an adrenaline-filled competition but also a Zen experience of awareness, connection, and growth.

Chapter 5. Beyond the Touchdown: Embracing the Transience of Victory

Early football games and those at the college level often had a simple scoring system: just one point could be chalked down for each goal. The game has rapidly evolved since its inception, and now a complex scoring system awards varying points based on how the goal was reached. Touchdowns are the most coveted - a glory that brings six points to the scoring team, providing a feeling of decisive victory.

Understanding and revelling in these wins is an integral part of the game, but with a Buddha-like perspective, we go further, embracing the transient nature of this victory.

5.1. The Impermanence of Glory

The Buddha often talked about the transient nature of life, that everything we cling to or chase is fleeting. This philosophy may seem somber or cynical at first glance, but when delved into deeper, it uncovers a profound way to live life – by embracing transiency and being fully present.

Every victory, just like the touchdown in a football game, is ephemeral. The exhilaration of a touchdown, the elation of the players, the euphoria of the cheering crowd, lasts only for that giddy moment. The scoreboard might stand witness to the conquest, but the moment itself slips away, giving way to the next play, the next attempt, the next struggle.

In stark contrast to the prevailing culture of celebrating big wins and milestones, this philosophy can appear counterproductive or even futile. However, there's a hidden wisdom in recognizing this transiency.

5.2. The Mindful Approach

Embracing impermanence is not about undermining the importance of or ignoring the thrill of conquest. Instead, it's a call to explore beyond the immediate. It places an emphasis on the moments that build up to the glory, both victories and failures.

When we imbibe this philosophy into our game, we deepen our connection to football. We celebrate the intricate dances of strategic planning, physical prowess, and perfect execution that constitutes these fleeting moments. We marvel at the passes, the blocks, the swift interlacing runs. We learn to appreciate every moment, and not just the touchdown.

5.3. Embracing the Journey

"Life is a journey. Time is a river. The door is ajar" - Jim Butcher.

We acknowledge this in our lives, yet we often tend to overlook this wisdom when it comes to football. We focus so much on the touchdown, the winning moment, that we might miss the beauty of the journey.

Every successful play is a byproduct of countless hours of practice, facing and overcoming physical and mental challenges, refining strategies, and enduring heartbreaks. This journey, much like life, ebbs and flows. By embracing the transience of victory, we stop living solely for the touchdown. We embrace the ebb and flow and, importantly, we enjoy every step.

5.4. Lessons From Losses

By focusing too much on victory and refusing to see beyond the touchdown, we risk falling into a dangerous trap. We may ignore the chance to learn, plummet into despair with loss, or even bask longer in the glory of a victory than necessary. This hinders both our growth and our enjoyment of the football game at hand.

Every missed pass, every toppled block, every failed strategy is a storehouse of valuable lessons. Through meditation and mindfulness, we can unearth these lessons, capitalize on them, and use them to enhance our future performances.

In conclusion, the spirit of Buddha's teachings beautifully connects with football when we visualize the sport beyond touchdowns, understanding that every victory or defeat is simply a stop in the long journey of the game. Embracing the transience of victory allows players to be more aligned with the present moment, practice sportsmanship, imbibe vital life lessons, focus on the journey, stay grounded, and learn from every game they play.

By revolutionizing our approach towards the game, we not only elevate our performance but also enrich our experience with football, transforming it from a string of isolated victories to an immersive, continuing journey.

Hence, Zen philosophy isn't about not engaging in the football game or scoring fewer touchdowns. On the contrary, it's about playing the game mindfully, focusing on the process as much as the result, and embracing each moment in its entirety. From this viewpoint, every pass, every block, every tackle takes on heightened significance, making the game more satisfying than ever.

Chapter 6. Mindful Drills: Training the Mind as Well as the Body

Football, a game of agility and strength, precision and strategy, is often considered solely a physical battleground. Champions are born in the gym, on the field, sweating under the weight of endless drills, scrimmages, and workouts. Yet, could there be an overlooked element, a resource untapped by the masses, one that is as essential as it is elusive? We propose that such an element exists, and it lies in training the mind.

6.1. The Power of Mindfulness

Mindfulness is the art of bringing one's attention to the present moment. It is to linger on the sensations, thoughts, and feelings that flow across the canvas of consciousness without judgement. Meditation is the workout with which this mindfulness muscle is fortified. By employing meditation, athletes can hone their focus, manage anxiety, visualize success, and maintain a level of self-awareness that optimally tunes the interior machinery.

To begin our journey towards the unique amalgamation of football and mindfulness, we start by understanding that these cogitative drills run parallel to physical drills. As with any good workout, we begin with a warm-up.

6.2. Warm-Up: Embracing Heraclitus's River

Every moment on the field is a droplet that merges into the river of

"

Heraclitus, where no one ever steps into the same river twice. For our mindful drills, the recognition and acceptance of this flux is the first step. The mindful warm-up involves a simple awareness meditation.

1. Sit comfortably and close your eyes.

2. Take a few deep breaths, focusing fully on the sensation of the air entering and leaving your body.

3. Guide your attention to the present moment. Notice any sensations, thoughts, or emotions that arise, without judgment.

4. When your mind wanders, gently guide it back to the present.

This primes your awareness muscle for the rest of the mindfulness drills.

6.3. Drill 1: Visualization

Visualization is a potent tool in the mindful arsenal, helping to evolve motor skills, refine strategies, and propel a player towards their goals.

1. Begin by closing your eyes and taking a few deep breaths.

2. Construct a clear image of your football field and position yourself there.

3. Play through some typical scenarios, focusing on your movements, actions, and the outcomes.

4. Once you gain comfort, visualize challenging and high-pressure situations and observe your virtual-self manage these successfully.

6.4. Drill 2: Mindful Breathing

Breathing is often autonomous, but focusing on this vital function brings a sense of calm and clarity.

1. Find a comfortable position and close your eyes.

2. Concentrate your attention on your breath. Notice the way air courses in and out of your body, the rise and fall of your chest.

3. Allow thoughts and sensations to arise, acknowledge them, and gently guide your attention back to your breath.

4. If you lose focus, gently return to the rhythm of your breath, fostering patience and concentration.

6.5. Drill 3: Body Scan

A body scan meditation encourages players to develop intricate awareness of their bodies, leading to better proprioception and injury prevention.

1. Lay down comfortably and close your eyes.

2. Beginning with your toes, gradually shift your attention up your body, lingering on each region to check in with how it feels.

3. Continue up to the crown of your head, focusing on releasing tension from each part.

4. As you finish your scan, take a few moments to sense and savor the entirety of your body.

6.6. Drill 4: Mindful Movement

This drill brings mindfulness into basic physical exercises, enhancing coordination and balance, and cultivating a deeper mind-muscle connection.

1. Start with a basic movement, like stretching or jogging.

2. Be fully conscious of each movement, each muscle's role. Feel

your body's response.

3. When your mind drifts, guide it back to the movement and bodily sensations.

6.7. Putting It All Together

Conduct these mindful drills alongside your regular physical exercises, and you should start to experience a new level of focus, resilience, and enhanced performance. Over time, incorporate mindfulness into actual game-play, noting each moment, fully immersing yourself in the ebb and flow of the game.

Thus, mental acuity and physical prowess converge on the football field, demonstrating that it's not just about overcoming the competitor but also about outdoing one's past self. It's harnessing the raw power of the moment, moment by moment, game after game. It's about defying Heraclitus's River, by stepping into the same river twice, thrice, ad infinitum, each time emerging as a better version of your former self; After all, bringing mindful tactics into your football study is stepping into the novel intersection of ancient wisdom and modern sport.

Chapter 7. Fumbles and Faults: Growing Through Setbacks

Football, in many ways, is a manifestation of life, full of triumphs, defeats, growth, and opportunities for learning. As in life, it's not about the setbacks we face - the fumbles and faults - but how we respond to them. How can we translate these moments into a vehicle for growth and transformation? That's where the Buddhist concept of mindfulness comes into play.

7.1. Embracing the Imperfections

Imperfections are woven into the fabric of existence. It's a universal truth, often overlooked, especially when observed through the lens of competitive sports, where perfection is revered and pursued relentlessly. No matter how skilled a player becomes or how flawless a team seems, a football game will always witness fumbles and faults. They are an inherent part of the game, and accepting them with grace is the first step towards growth.

The teachings of the Buddha emphasize acceptance, a meditation practice called vipassana or mindfulness, which encourages us to accept the situation for what it is. When a fumble occurs or a fault happens, rather than resist it, we bless it, embrace it, and learn from it. It's not about making them vanish but to observe them, discern their causes, and extract lessons from them to inform future actions.

7.2. The Nature of Suffering (Dukkha)

Fumbles and faults cause us suffering – emotional and psychological pain. But suffering, as the Buddha taught, is a part of life. It's a veil that obscures our true nature, yet it's also the tool we can use to transcend our limitations. When we understand the root cause of our suffering, we are able to overcome it. The same applies to fumbles and faults on the playing field.

In the context of football, fumbles and faults often stem from fear, tension, distraction, poor preparation, or simply a lack of skill. The first noble truth, the truth of dukkha (suffering), invites us to face our emotions head-on. We consciously observe our feelings of frustration, embarrassment, or disappointment that arise from these setbacks. By acknowledging these emotions rather than avoiding them, we begin to dissipate their power over us.

7.3. The "Middle Path" to Tackling Setbacks

How should we navigate our way through these challenging moments? The Buddha's 'Middle Path' suggests a balanced response. It does not promote dwelling in negativity and self-criticism nor falling into apathy or indifference. Instead, one should imbibe a growth mindset, a peaceful acceptance of the situation, coupled with the intention to improve.

On the football field, this translates into studying the reasons behind the fumble or fault, developing strategies to improve, and working persistently towards implementing these strategies. Were you not focused enough? Practice mindfulness exercises to enhance concentration. Was your technique flawed? Seek mentorship from a coach to refine it.

This constant loop of mindful observation, acceptance, learning, and improvement embodies the spirit of Buddha's teachings, bringing profound insight and personal growth from the simplest of fumbles to the most glaring of faults.

7.4. Developing Equanimity

Buddhism advocates maintaining equanimity or remaining calm and composed in all situations, viewing success and failure as two sides of the same coin. It's about learning to maintain your composure, irrespective of the outcome on the field.

By viewing your fumbles and faults through a lens of equanimity, frees your mind from the torment of dwelling in setbacks. Remember, equanimity does not mean lack of passion or drive for improvement. Rather, it encourages us to have an unwavering attitude, undeterred by setbacks.

7.5. Transformation through Mindfulness

Mindfulness is the cornerstone of Buddhism. It is about being conscious of our thoughts, feelings, and actions in a non-judgmental and compassionate way. The application of mindfulness to fumbles and faults on the football field can lead to transformative growth.

Each time a fumble or fault occurs, treat it as an opportunity for mindfulness. Observe the event without judgment, identifying the reasons that led to it. Was it a lapse in concentration, a gap in skills, or a lack of readiness? By being mindful, you can identify the actual triggers behind your setbacks. After acknowledging these triggers, work to address them thoughtfully, with acceptance and commitment to self-improvement.

Buddha's teachings reflect the wisdom that all experiences, pleasant and unpleasant, are opportunities for growth and self-realization. When we apply these teachings to football, especially in dealing with fumbles and faults, we will not only become better players, but our love for the game will also flourish. We will learn how to turn our setbacks into springboards for profound personal and mental growth. Ultimately, we will enrich our experience of the great game of football, making it a mindful, soulful, and transformative journey.

Chapter 8. Huddle and Dharma: The Power of Team Unity

In the realm of football, one of the most critical moments of any game is the huddle. It's not just a quick gathering of teammates. It's an integral center of communication, strategy planning, and shared commitment. Arguably, the huddle showcases the essence of the team as a whole, and it corresponds closely to the Buddhist concept of 'Dharma', or duty in unity and harmony.

8.1. The Indispensable Huddle

Football, by its very nature, is a team sport requiring extensive coordination and communication. A huddle is where this team interaction predominantly occurs. In a huddle, each player steps outside of their individuality and becomes, truly, a part of the team. They share information, strategize, and prepare for the impending play, all while focusing on their interdependent roles and objectives.

The silence amidst the roaring crowds, the eye contact among teammates, the weighty words of the quarterback delivering the play - these elements weave a powerful tableau of unity and prepare the team for their ensuing actions on the field.

8.2. Dharma: The Buddhist Concept of Unity and Duty

Antiquated as it may be, the Buddhist concept of Dharma provides a unique lens through which we can view the huddle dynamics. 'Dharma' refers to the duties, rights, laws, conducts, virtues and 'the right way of living'. In Buddhist philosophy, it implies duty in unity, serving to maintain and promote harmony in the universe.

Dharma insists that all things and beings are interconnected. In essence, each individual's Dharma, or duty, is shaped by their relationships and connections to the world around them. A person's Dharma balances their individual needs with the greater good, creating a harmony that supports not just the individual, but all connected entities.

8.3. Drawing Parallels: Huddle and Dharma

At a glance, Dharma and huddles are two drastically different concepts. Yet, they share an underlying similarity: the emphasis on unity and shared responsibility. Both enforce the understanding that the whole is far greater than the sum of its parts.

In a team huddle, as in the practice of Dharma, players learn to set aside their individual identities, focusing instead on their duties and roles within the team. They understand that their collective goal—scoring a touchdown or halting the opposing offense—is larger than their individual ambitions. Similarly, in Dharma, the larger cosmic order takes precedence over individual desires.

The huddle is a moment of unity, collaboration, and shared commitment mirroring the spirit of Dharma. It embodies the belief that together, the team is more potent, more balanced, and more likely to overcome any challenge thrown their way.

8.4. Mindfulness in the Huddle

Using mindfulness, players can further enhance the power of the huddle. Mindfulness—the act of fully focusing on the present moment with acceptance—allows athletes to engage more deeply in their surroundings, promotes clearer communication, and fosters greater unity within the team.

By practicing mindfulness in the huddle, players can hone their focus, listen more effectively, and better understand their roles. The execution of the gameplan becomes smoother and more efficient. Anxiety and impatience give way to calm and composed action.

8.5. Applying the Philosophies

The interconnection of Dharma and the football huddle can be further extended to everyday life. Just like the various positions in football, our roles in families, communities, or workplaces entail certain duties that contribute to an overarching goal. By embracing Dharma's teachings, we can work harmoniously in a united way, fulfilling our tasks effectively—proving that the essence and power of Dharma can be found just as much in everyday life as in a football huddle.

Indeed, whether it's on the game field or the field of life, the principles encapsulated in the Buddhist Dharma can help us all to function as better team players, fostering unity and harmony. Thus, the philosophy of 'Huddle and Dharma' is not a mere intellectual curiosity—it's a practical tool, a way to infuse our approach to team situations with mindfulness and unity, whether that's in a spirited game of football or the broader game of life.

Chapter 9. Observing the Breath, Observing the Game: The Art of Active Awareness

The connection between the breath and the game may seem tenuous to some. How could a natural process seemingly unlinked to the rough and tumble of football teach us anything about the sport itself? Delving into the Buddha's teachings, though, reveals the answer. Not only does the breath serve as an anchor, tethering us to the present moment, but also mirrors the elements of dynamism, rhythm, and mindfulness present in football.

Starting with a simple mindful breathing exercise can help establish this connection. Sit in a comfortable position, close your eyes, and focus on your breath. Notice how it ebbs and flows, much like the rhythm of a football game. You'll feel inhalation like a buildup of a play, exhalation like its execution, and the pause as the moment of suspense before the cycle begins anew.

9.1. Cultivating Mindfulness

Mindfulness is the quality of being present and fully engaged in whatever you're doing, free from distraction or judgment, and with a soft and open mind. The first step in cultivating mindfulness is through attentive breathing, aligning your consciousness with the rhythm of your breath.

In football, mindfulness relates to being fully present on the field. It involves understanding the situation, knowing the position of each player, predicting the opponent's moves, and coordinating your own. The quarterback must be mindful of the current game situation, his teammates' positions, and the opponents' potential tactics. His effectiveness depends on his mindful awareness of the present moment.

Likewise, by bringing our attention back to the breath, time and again, we engage the mind fully in the present moment. Thoughts of the past or future are recognized as distractions, gently set aside, and we return to the breath.

9.2. Breathing and Responding, Not Reacting

In football, the ability to react quickly is often praised. Yet the wisdom of Buddha differentiates between a reactive mind, shaped by habits and patterns, and a responsive mind, malleable and adaptable. The breath, with its cyclical nature, offers the perfect training ground for this skill.

When you begin your mindful breathing, there might be an urge to control it. Resist this urge and observe the breath without interfering. The instruction is not to breathe in a particular way but to bear faithful witness to it. Your mind will likely wander - that's perfectly normal. But each time it strays, just notice where it went, then gently escort it back to your breath.

Similarly, in football, many situations will evoke a typical reaction. A tight end seeing an open field in front of him might instinctively sprint full speed ahead, potentially overlooking other strategic maneuvers. When we observe and become familiar with our go-to reactions, we can then choose a more mindful, considered response instead. Training your attention through breath enables you to spot these habitual reactions, disarm them, and freely choose your response.

9.3. Breath as the Game's Rhythm

The cyclical nature of the breath mirrors the dynamics of a football game. For instance, in a game, there are periods of intense action and periods of relative calm.

Just like each part of the breathing cycle serves a purpose, each phase of the game holds its significance. Some moments might seem less eventful – during a timeout, for example – yet they provide opportunities to slow down, strategize, and gather your strength, much like the pause in the breath cycle.

9.4. Mindful Breathing, Mindful Playing

Just as the breath flows in and out, football is an ebb and flow of offense and defense, movement and pause. Practice mindful breathing daily, and apply the same principles to your game. Watch the patterns emerge, observe the play, remain aware but non-judgmental. With more understanding, patterns unfold, and soon you'll find yourself intuitively 'in sync' with the game. You'll be more balanced, more adaptable, and more attuned to the unfolding dynamic of the football field.

9.5. Concluding Remarks: Breath, the Game, and Life

The practice of mindful breathing illuminates the path to mindful awareness, not only for football but also for life's pursuits. Just as we train ourselves to come back to our breath, we must remind ourselves to come back to the present moment in life.

Observing the breath is not about achieving a 'zen' state or unlocking hidden mystical potential. It is about being fully in touch with the present moment, acknowledging it, understanding it, and living it to the fullest.

So, the next time you watch or play a game of football, imbibe the qualities of the breath into the game. Observe the rhythm, maintain consistent awareness, be flexible, and choose responses over reactions. Remember that, like the breath, the game is fleeting, transient, and cyclical – and it is therein its beauty lies. Through this realignment, you'll not only gain a newfound appreciation for the 'beautiful game,' but also find a more mindful, present, and authentic way to live. Whether on the field or in life, the mindful experience is yours to seize, breathe by breath, play by play.

Chapter 10. Turning Penalties into Progress: Applying the Middle Way

Football, just like life, is filled with moments of triumph and defeat, ebbs and flows of hope and despair, instantaneous reversals of fortune. It is during these trying times that we often find ourselves lashing out, losing our cool, drawing penalties. But what if, instead of viewing these penalties as setbacks, we looked at them through the lens of the Buddha's Middle Path? The Middle Way, often interpreted to mean "moderation", refers to a balanced approach to life symbolizing the cultivation of wisdom. The philosophy encourages a healthy balance between two extremes - indulgence and deprivation. Now let's see how we can apply this to football, specifically for turning penalties into progress.

10.1. Cultivating Acceptance

In the face of penalties, the first instinct often is to lash out, curse, or blame either oneself or the team member responsible for the infringement. Much like the perennial struggle of human beings oscillating between highs and lows, players can become entangled in a cycle of self-blame and frustration. The Middle Way asks that we approach these instances with acceptance.

The key is not to be indifferent towards penalties but to accept them as a part of the game's dynamic flux, much like the obstacles we face in life. Remind yourself that losing yourself in the anger and frustration of a penalty only hinders your focus, disrupts the team's synergy and adds no value to your performance or the match's outcome.

10.2. The Middle Path Between Complacency and Recklessness

Another footprint of the Middle Way lies in maintaining equilibrium between recklessness and complacency. Often players can be excessively aggressive, risking penalties, or overly cautious, hindering the game's flow—both extremes cause imbalance.

The Middle Way asks us to maintain a careful balance between aggression and restraint on the field, playing assertively yet mindfully. Aggression fuels forward movement and propels us to take risks, while restraint helps keep the game's rules intact. Striving for this balance will enhance your gameplay, reducing the probability of penalties.

10.3. The Power of Awareness

The Buddha's teachings highlight the importance of awareness in achieving a balanced life. Football, being a game much about mindfulness as physical skill, requires that we bring our full attention to each moment.

Awareness is specifically crucial when it comes to penalties, often stemming from lack of attention to the rules or the game's current flow. By developing mindfulness, players can avoid unnecessary penalties and improve their performance on the field.

10.4. Utilizing Penalties for Positive Reinforcement

Training the mind to embrace mistakes as learning opportunities is a cornerstone of the Buddha's Middle Way. Every time a penalty is committed, see it as an opportunity to learn, grow, and improve.

Turning penalties into progress is not just about preventing their occurrence but also turning them into triggers for positive reinforcement. Players can reflect on what led to the penalty and devise strategies to prevent them in the future. This positive-education approach also eliminates the fear and negativity surrounding penalties, thus promoting resilience and contributing to personal growth.

10.5. Managing Emotional Extremes on the Field

The Middle Way can be fundamental in managing the emotional extremes on the field. The highs of a touchdown or the lows of a foul shouldn't dictate your emotional state. Rather, maintaining an even keel allows you to handle every situation with equilibrium.

It's impossible to prevent penalties in every game, but with the Middle Way's application, they can become a tool for progress and improvement. The Buddha's teachings provide a framework that proves invaluable not only on the field but throughout life.

10.6. Peak Performance: A Perfect Balance

In the end, it all boils down to balance. Balancing aggression and caution, accepting situations and taking steps to improve, staying focused and detached all at once, and using penalties as a tool for positive reinforcement are all facets of the Middle Way that can be applied to football.

It's about balance, fair play, sportsmanship, and an enlightened perspective on the gridiron. The Middle Way leads to a harmonious blend of mental and physical strength, discipline and spontaneity, competitiveness and respect - the essentials for elevating any game.

And when it comes to football, this approach can indeed turn penalties into progress and model an enriched way of meeting life's challenges.

This chapter might feel like an unexpected summer shower, washing away the dust of entrenched perspectives. If so, then it's accomplished its purpose. You're invited to take these lessons and carry them with you onto the field. As you do, you'll observe a subtle but profound shift in how you play, how you view penalties, and ultimately, how you participate and progress in the beautiful game of football.

Chapter 11. Post-Game Meditation: Reflections on the Essence of Impermanence

After the dust of battle has settled, the noise of the crowd has filtered out into silence, and the adrenaline rush has subsided, it's easy to retreat into a mental replay of the game, fixating on mistakes made, victories won, or chances missed. Yet, such an approach frequently misses the ephemeral beauty of the game and its inherent teachings. It is here we introduce the concept of post-game meditation, leveraging football as a metaphorical ground to understand the essence of impermanence - a profound teaching of Buddha.

11.1. Embracing Impermanence, in Football and Life

Football, much like life, is a dance of impermanence. The thrill of a touchdown or intercept is as fleeting as the despair of a lost match or an inaccurate pass. Meditating on the similarity between these transitory highs and lows in football, and the ever-transforming nature of life facilitates acceptance of change. As we understand the ephemeral, we unlock deeper layers of mindfulness and acceptance, learning to proverbially 'go with the flow.' This acceptance begins with observing and unifying with the rhythm of impermanence.

Take each game encounter as a series of experiential landscapes. From boot strike to end whistle, myriad unanticipated events occur—triumphs, downfalls, twists, and turns. Recognize these as part of the game's fluid trajectory and allow them to flow freely. Incorporate into your meditation an acknowledgement of each significant encounter from the game: the rush of scoring, the heartbreak of a near miss, the ebbs and flows of teamwork on the field.

11.2. Incorporating Impermanence into Meditation: A Practical Guide

Post-game reflection is some of the richest ground on which to cultivate mindful acceptance of transience. This becomes less about team-centric victories or losses and more about embracing the organic flow of experiences.

Begin by finding a quiet space that promotes reflection. Bring your mind's attention to your breath. Breathe in deeply, hold for a few seconds, exhale fully. Repeat this cycle, anchoring your thoughts to your conscious breathing. As you navigate this mindful space, begin to replay the game within your mental arena.

For each significant event, consciously perceive it as a fluid moment, existing for a while, then replaced by the next event - much like waves on a beach retreating to bring forth a new one. Pause and embrace each moment as it was: exhilarating, heartbreaking, triumphant, teaching. Let emotions wash over you like waves, coming and going, teaching acceptance in their wake. Allow yourself to live in each instance, again and again, grounding in the poignant impermanence each moment symbolizes.

11.3. From Acceptance to Insight: Nurturing Growth and Resilience

Post-game meditation isn't merely an exercise towards gentle acceptance. It's a tool that fosters growth and resilience. As we mindfully embrace the changing panorama of the game, understanding that nothing is ever statically victorious or defeating, we carry this lesson into broader life.

Apply the practice of seeing impermanence in the way you approached the game, or how you responded to an opponent's move. Meditate on how you used strategies, thinking about how they were successful or unsuccessful, and why. Much like the strategic moves in the game, life, too, is a series of decisions we make. The outcomes are transient, constantly shifting. Understand that both victory and defeat are temporary states, and they do not define you as a player or a person.

11.4. Coming into Being: The Zen of Football

The culmination of post-game meditation is- coming into a state of 'being,' embodying the teachings of the Buddha, and translating them onto the football field. This exploration isn't merely about performance enhancement but a holistic exploration of football as a physical, mental, and spiritual practice.

Just as the game evolves play after play, we too must learn to understand, adapt, and navigate the fluid landscape of existence, whether it is on or off the field. By performing this post-game meditation consistently, one begins to find peace amidst chaos, acceptance in change, and an opportunity for growth in every game's end. Trust this: Nothing is permanent in football, life, or this universe, and therein lies its beauty.

Thus, the Zen of football becomes a potent blend of athletic precision, mental acuity, and spiritual wisdom. It's not only about being a mindful football player. It's about being a mindful 'being.' It's not just playing football, it's playing the symphony of life - with all its unpredictable rhythms and intricate dynamics.

So we say, let impermanence into your game. Welcome it. Embrace it. Learn from it. Draw wisdom from its teaching. For impermanence is not the end game, just another play in the grand scheme of things.

Cherish it, flow with it, and let it flow through you. As you step back into life, or onto the field for your next match, carry this enlightened perspective with you – the mindful recognition of the breathtaking impermanence within the game of football, and indeed, life itself.